A Crabtree Roots Book

It's Chinese New Year!

My Favorite Holiday

AMY CULLIFORD

Crabtree Publishing
crabtreebooks.com

School-to-Home Support for Caregivers and Teachers

This book helps children grow by letting them practice reading. Here are a few guiding questions to help the reader build his or her comprehension skills. Possible answers appear here in red.

Before Reading:

- What do I think this book is about?
    - *I think this book is about the Chinese New Year.*
    - *I think this book is about children in Chinese New Year parades.*
- What do I want to learn about this topic?
    - *I want to learn more about why the Chinese New Year is celebrated.*
    - *I want to learn about the costumes people wear on the Chinese New Year.*

During Reading:

- I wonder why...
    - *I wonder why the January 1st New Year is different from the Chinese New Year.*
    - *I wonder why there are so many red lanterns hung for the Chinese New Year.*
- What have I learned so far?
    - *I have learned that there is usually a Chinese New Year parade.*
    - *I have learned that fireworks are set off during the Chinese New Year.*

After Reading:

- What details did I learn about this topic?
    - *I have learned that there are many red lanterns everywhere on the Chinese New Year.*
    - *I have learned that some people give gifts on the Chinese New Year.*
- Read the book again and look for the vocabulary words.
    - *I see the word **parade** on page 8 and the word **fireworks** on page 12. The other vocabulary words are found on page 14.*

It is **Chinese New Year!**

I see red all around.

I open a **gift**!

I see a **parade**.

There are many red **lanterns**.

I see **fireworks**!

Word List

Sight Words

a	I	open
all	is	red
are	it	see
around	many	there

Words to Know

Chinese New Year

fireworks

gift

lanterns

parade

26 Words

It is **Chinese New Year**!

I see red all around.

I open a **gift**!

I see a **parade**.

There are many red **lanterns**.

I see **fireworks**!

It's Chinese New Year!

My Favorite Holiday

Crabtree Publishing

crabtreebooks.com 800-387-7650

In Canada: We acknowledge the financial support of the Government of Canada through the Canada Book Fund for our publishing activities.

Hardcover 978-1-0396-5973-5
Paperback 978-1-0396-6168-4
Ebook (pdf) 978-1-0396-6964-2
Epub 978-1-0396-7162-1
Read-along 978-1-0396-7360-1
Audio book 978-1-0396-7558-2

Library and Archives Canada Cataloguing in Publication
Available at the Library and Archives Canada

Library of Congress Cataloging-in-Publication Data
Available at the Library of Congress

Published in Canada
Crabtree Publishing
616 Welland Avenue
St. Catharines, Ontario
L2M 5V6

Published in the United States
Crabtree Publishing
347 Fifth Avenue
Suite 1402-145
New York, NY 10016

Written by: Amy Culliford
Designed by: Bobbie Houser
Series Development: James Earley
Proofreader: Petrice Custance
Educational Consultant: Marie Lemke M.Ed.
Production manager: Candice Campbell

Photographs: t = Top, c = Center, b = Bottom, l = Left, r = Right; Shutterstock: asharkyu: cover; alexan888: p. 1; KeongDaGreat: p. 3, 14; Sofiaworld: p. 5 tl; wong yu liang: p. 5 tr; Sergei Bachlakov: p. 5 b; JenJ_Payless: p. 6, 14; cowardlion: p. 9, 14; Ekkalak Ngamjarasvanij: p. 10, 14; Krunja: p. 12-14

Printed in the U.S.A./CP032026